Fundamentals of World Building

Jessie Verino

L & L Dreamspell
Spring, Texas

Cover and Interior Design by L & L Dreamspell

ISBN: 978-1-60318-172-3

Visit us on the web at www.lldreamspell.com

Published by L & L Dreamspell
Printed in the United States of America

Contents

Introduction: The Tapestry

World building is so much more than creating a planet in a galaxy far, far away. Writers must take the foreign, the alien, the unfamiliar, and make it resonate with readers. Readers should feel welcome in the world created, not like an outsider or a spectator. They need to identify with the characters, be they humanoid, demon, angel, vampire, were, or an alien form of life.

Simply stated, the writer must make the unbelievable believable.

In the world of speculative fiction, it's not only important to have a great story, it's imperative to have a great story world. A thinly veiled version of life on Earth, either from the 12th century or the current century, will read exactly like what it is—an artless and amateurish attempt. Readers won't accept the work, no matter how well the author has crafted the plot, if the story world doesn't enhance the story to its fullest potential.

The story world must be as fully developed as the characters and the plot. Even a world of chaos must be structured and fleshed out in such a way that the reader can relate and fully immerse himself in the world. Readers need to feel at home in the story world, whether it's another planet or another dimension.

Balance is the key. The story world should not overwhelm the story. Nor should it linger around the edges of the story, creeping in only when needed to explain a story element. Story and story world should be an intricately woven tapestry, each thread dependent on the other to present the whole pattern. Any bare spot, any frayed edge, any torn or faded thread will ruin the aesthetic value of the art.

To build a story world, the author must be part artist, part engineer, and sometimes part mad scientist. Elements need to be built and structured with the greatest attention to detail and then painted with the visionary's palette.

This is not intended to be a complete reference, a compendium of world-building knowledge, or even how to write a speculative fiction novel (although bits of character development, plot development, and conflict may sneak in while the story world is under construction). It is a starting point and quick reference guide to the construction of a story world, the elements that comprise the different types of world, and how those elements interact to create a believable story world.

Before You Begin: The Story Bible

Some writers keep a story world notebook, commonly referred to as a bible, to keep track of their world elements. I strongly recommend this method. If using a spiral bound notebook, purchase one that has dividers, such as a five-subject notebook, to keep your information organized.

If you decide to purchase a three-ring binder, be sure to purchase a set of dividers, preferably with pockets, or letter-sized manila folders. I have found the folders work well if you want to remove one portion of the information and work on it without the clumsiness of a notebook. Labels can include characters (major and minor), places, transportation, clothing, magic spells, maps, rituals, plot points, secrets, or anything the writer deems important about the story world. Color folders are also available for color-coding.

Pocket dividers can hold bits of information you acquire from magazine or newspaper articles or the Internet, as well as photographs, maps, or ideas scribbled on a napkin during lunch. Sheet protectors are also a good idea if you plan on using full-page articles, maps, or large photographs, as they will protect those items from being lost, stained, or torn.

Of course, pocket dividers, sheet protectors, and pouches (for pens and holding note and idea cards) can be used with the folder method. Use whatever works and fits with your writing style.

Another route, if you're comfortable with having the information on the Internet as opposed to hard copy, is to create your own world-building wiki. Several websites offer free wikis. Some even have a wiki that will transfer to a hard drive or a USB drive for portability. Wikis are a good place to store a lot of information. In any search engine, type the words, "free wiki." A list of several sites will be at your fingertips. Be sure to check them out thoroughly and choose one that best fits your needs. If you want to have parts of your wiki private and parts of it public, be certain you can create both public and private pages before you start adding information.

A word of caution. No matter how you keep your story world information organized, make copies and backups.

One
What is a Story World?

In the most simple terms, the story world is the setting in which the story takes place, whether it be outer space, a lost city such as Atlantis, or an alternate or parallel universe. However, setting is the broad stroke of the brush, the background for the details that bring the story to life.

Clothing, architecture, weather, terrain, vehicles, furniture, types of energy, and art are only a few of the minute details that will decorate the story world.

The story usually starts with a "what if" scenario and so does the story world. The "what if" scenarios that drive most story tellers usually involve characters or character types. What if the vampire hunter fell in love with his quarry? What if the wizard lost his magical ability as the forces of darkness invaded his home?

Even those scenarios that don't start with a character quickly bring characters to the forefront. What if aliens invaded Earth? The writer would probably build a resistance group. What if the sun suddenly started dying? The writer would probably build a scientific team and an astronaut mission team. Therefore, the rich, vibrant details that make a story memorable are related to the characters, their conflicts and emotions, not just the setting.

In order to build the story world, it is the world builder's job to ask "why" in conjunction with "what if." The question might have more than one answer. First would be the obvious answer, which is apparent almost from page one. Then would come the deeper, more complex answer from the story world's mythology and the character's goals, motivation, and conflict, which comes to light as the story develops.

Why is the hunter after the vampire? The immediate answer: Because the vampire killed or turned a close friend. The story world mythology answer: The vampires were the indigenous species of the world and the human race was created as the result of a scientific experiment in hopes of curing some disease. When the humans became sentient, they were treated as lab rats, then as slaves. Eventually the humans rebelled and the vampires were forced into their now secret societies in order to survive. There is still a deep hatred between the vampires and the humans.

Why are dark forces invading the wizard's world? The immediate answer: There is something in the wizard's world the dark forces need, like water, or a certain mineral, or a power source. The story world mythology answer: Eons ago, a powerful wizard predicted that a race from another world would harness the unknown power of some sacred source. In fear, the other races tried to annihilate them before the prediction could come true. Those actions of others have turned the race dark and bitter. Now, they travel to the wizard's world for a final showdown, to obtain the sacred source, and a possibly a new prediction.

Why are aliens invading? The immediate answer: To conquer humans and use humans as slaves. The story world mythology answer: Before the Dark Ages, humans had the secrets of space flight but unintentionally caused the death of a member of the royal family of the invading force's home planet, as well as a rift in space/time that caused Earth to plummet into the Dark Ages. As a result, the people of Earth forgot their technology. The rift has now been repaired, and the invaders are able to take their revenge.

Why is the sun dying? The immediate answer: Its supply of hydrogen is running out faster than scientists first thought. The story world mythology answer: A curse uttered in a moment of madness by a sorcerer.

The answers to these questions are also the beginning of the story world mythology and where the real world building takes place.

The mindset of the characters, the way they think and approach problems, is probably one of the most telling ways a writer relates the mythology to the reader. If the character believes in the omniscience of a religious figure (i.e., God will provide), with the utmost sincerity of the fanatic believer, and to the point where the character looks to a higher power to provide guidance in all things, the reader can deduce that this is a world where religion rules all aspects of life. Of course, there is also the opposite. The reader can also understand the same circumstances from a character who despises the religious beliefs being forced upon the people and fights to end religious absolutism.

Customs are also a way for the writer to sneak in a bit of the world's mythology. The most common custom is some form of greeting, whether it is a handshake, a hug, a kiss, a bow, or something else. The greeting custom usually dates back thousands of years in a society's mythology and can have different meanings at different times.

For instance, a handshake can be an informal hello type greeting between friends or a more formal hello type greeting between business associates. For those not quite friends or enemies, the force and strength of the handshake may relay information. One theory states, the handshake developed between possible combatants to show they were unarmed when they approached. The handshake can be used to seal a deal, like a spit-shake, or to seal a fate as when the palms are cut and the blood of the palms is mixed during the handshake ritual. This type of weaving in small bits of mythology can be very telling to the reader.

Character ability will also stem from the story world mythology. A certain group of vampires may have the ability to fly while others do not. A psychic ability may have been given to a favored woman from a god or supernatural force and passed down for generations through maternal genetics. A society formed in an undersea landscape may have the ability to breath underwater as well as on land. A short sentence or paragraph can be used to explain certain society or character abilities without having to write an entire history.

The one common element of the examples given is the writer's ability to show these as action. In the religion example, the reader need only "hear" the character say "God will provide" once, either spoken or in thought. However, if every time the character sees some sort of religious symbol, he stops and makes the required gesture of faith, whether or not anyone is there to witness it, the reader can deduce the importance.

There are several other aspects to building a world. The development of weaponry, magic, technology, and superstitions all play a part. So, we move from the most simple definition of story world as setting to the realization that everything is part of the story world.

The artist persona of the world builder must create the background. The engineer persona of the world builder must find a way to present each facet of the world as a seamless part of the whole. The mad scientist persona will add the quirky touches of character personality and the unique style of everyday items such as clothing, architecture, and furniture.

To accomplish all of these things, the world builder needs a set of blueprints.

Two
The Blueprints

Just as a construction crew wouldn't build a house without a set of blueprints, an author shouldn't try to build a story world without them. Each blueprint in the set will contain the basic shape and size of the building. One blueprint will have the foundation specifications, one will have the interior walls, doors, and windows marked. One blueprint will have the electrical diagrams, and another will have plumbing diagrams. To build a story world, the writer needs a full set of blueprints.

The writer is the architect of the story and therefore is also the creator of the blueprints. This is where the story bible, along with the world-building worksheet, can be of immense help.

One of my father's maxims was, "Pencils are made for remembering." He tended to say this more often when he was giving me directions for some task, as he was not content to rely on my memory and had me write things down. As I matured, I realized this maxim fit more areas of my life than Dad's directions, or notes for a test, or even a grocery list. If I don't write something down, I will invariably forget it. The same holds true for story world details.

I use manila folders in a notebook as my story world bible. I have a folder for characters, one for landscapes, one for plot, one for mythology, one for descriptions, and so on. And I use my pencil, or my computer printout, or photograph, for remembering.

The blueprints may encompass the whole of the story world, or one set of blueprints may be created for a city, state, or region.

The story world may require several sets of blueprints, depending on the number of physical locations in the story and the number of different societies. However, don't let the idea of creating several sets of blueprints become intimidating. The world building worksheet is for jotting down initial thoughts for later expansion, and the story bible is to keep those thoughts organized.

I recommend building from the smallest story world to the universal story world. If the story is a space epic, the task of fitting smaller worlds, such as several different planets, into a universe that has already been fully fleshed out and built is harder than structuring the universe around the smaller worlds.

The sections of the world-building worksheet correspond to the different blueprints, and unfortunately a lot, or most, of the information asked for on the worksheet will not actually be used in the story. However, the information is necessary for the writer to develop a clear vision of the story world and to relate the vision into words.

Of course, building a world is a little more complex than building a house. And while there is a certain order to building any structure, including a story world, sometimes deviations need to be made. There is no right way or wrong order to building a story world, and the order I present is what works for me. I believe a writer should use the most effective way for his/her writing personality. I start with landscaping.

Three
The Landscape

To have the correct set of blueprints, the writer needs to know the type of world to be built. Most worlds in speculative fiction can be categorized as one of the following:

- Alternate Dimension/Alternate Universe
- Alternate History
- Alternate Reality/Parallel Universe/Multiverse
- Fantasy
- Science Fiction
- Shadow
- Virtual Reality
- Earth
- Time Travel

And, of course, there are subcategories within the categories. The types of worlds can, and often do, overlap. The key to blending two or more worlds is balance. Some elements from a fantasy world may fit well in a science fiction world, but building a world with several elements from different types of worlds will result in something grotesque and unrecognizable. Readers won't suspend their disbelief for a story that has them jumping from medieval to space to fairy rings to avatars. The writer should try to stay with a basic structure until they have built a few successful story worlds and have discovered through their own voice and writing style which elements mix well with others.

Which world to choose? The best fit for the characters, your knowledge, or your ability to research the knowledge needed, and the time period (historical, contemporary, futuristic, or a mixture through time-travel). Or, if the characters have not shown themselves yet, choose a world that is personally appealing and intriguing.

Once the type of world is determined, a proper set of blue prints can be drawn.

Please note—these are my interpretations of the story worlds and the different types of elements that comprise them.

The Alternate Dimension/Alternate Universe

An alternate dimension is a world outside the space/time of our universe. Scientists have speculated that there may be as many as eleven dimensions, including those we recognize as width, depth, height, and time. Alternate dimensions are where the experienced world builder can have fun, and the beginning world builder can experiment. These worlds are a playground for the imagination. Any type of world can be constructed in an alternate dimension, or a mixture of worlds and creatures.

In an alternate dimension, the laws of science and physics as we understand them need not apply. For example, the sun in an alternate dimension may produce a cold light. However, the laws and rules the writer establishes must be adhered to throughout the story. They cannot be changed for convenience if they conflict with a part of the plot.

The story may start in an alternate dimension with characters moving from one alternate dimension to another, or the writer can transport the characters to another dimension from Earth. Transporting characters from one alternate dimension to another takes some care, along with a source of energy with enough power to pull the characters from one dimension to another. Unfortunately, it is also more than enough power to kill the characters. It is the writer's job to set up the rules and give a plausible explanation as to why the characters were able to survive the energy. It should be so seamlessly woven into the characters, the plot, and the world that the reader's suspension of disbelief is maintained. The writer does not want the reader to stop and question the how and why of an element of the story world.

It has been suggested that dreams are also portals to an alternate dimension as they often have elements that defy the physical universe as we know it. A psychic character, or a character who has latent psychic ability, might enter an alternate dimension through a dream portal. Things to consider with this scenario are whether the character can control travel between dimensions through dreams, and whether the character can contact others who do not have psychic ability and take them through the portal by entering the other character's dreams.

Whichever mode of transport the writer decides to use, it must be logical in the confines of the story and story world.

Alternate History

An alternate history story is much more than taking a historical fact and changing it to fit a story. Cause and effect should be taken into consideration. If the Boston Tea Party had never occurred, would there still have been a Revolutionary War? These stories require a lot of research, not only of the events to be changed, but what those events affected and the results. Also, the alternate results should have a reasonable theory to justify them.

Alternate Reality/Parallel Universe/Multiverse

An alternate reality, sometimes referred to as a parallel universe, differs from an alternate dimension. Where the physical laws of science need not apply in an alternate dimension, they do apply in an alternate reality. In essence, an alternate reality or parallel universe is our world in a different timeline. Suppose Germany, or even a country that was neutral in our history, like

Argentina, had won World War II. Suppose a meteor had never hit the Earth and caused the Ice Age. What if electricity had never been discovered, or penicillin? According to theory, these are realities in parallel universes. The term multiverse is used when referencing all possible scenarios to consist of all reality.

A word of caution, here. A different timeline in the sense that an event happened that wasn't supposed to happen, or an event that was supposed to happen never happened, is different than events that take place in another dimension outside the space/ time of our universe. If it's 2008 when the character enters the alternate reality, it will still be 2008 in the alternate reality. The flow of time doesn't change, only the events.

The characters may start in their own reality and travel to ours, or vice-versa. However, it is the point of an alternate reality world to show the differences in the realities. Otherwise, the story is simply an alternate history story.

Fantasy

The classic sword and sorcery story, often referred to as high fantasy, is set in a world where the women are fair, the men are heroes, and the black knight or evil wizard is set on destroying them all. The fantasy world contains magic in all its forms: white magic, black magic, and earth magic, as well as alchemy. Magic is an accepted part of the everyday life in a fantasy world. However, the magic bestowed on a character through the plot often comes with a price or consequences not expected by the characters.

Life in the high fantasy world is simple with very little technology and often resembles Europe in the Middle Ages. The main characters are often called upon to perform some heroic deed, or they may be called upon to journey on a quest either to win a great prize, or to save the kingdom.

In the fantasy story world, more so than the other story worlds, the inhabitants are integral. A fantasy world will have castles, unicorns, fairies, witches, wizards, alchemists, trolls, angels, etc. These inhabitants will live, for the most part, in harmony with the human inhabitants. In contrast, dark fantasy will have vampires, demons, dragons, werewolves, gargoyles, harpies, and other assorted beasts and monsters. The tone of dark fantasy may drift to horror, and there is conflict with the human inhabitants.

The urban fantasy story world has many of the same elements of the high fantasy or dark fantasy story, only these stories take place on Earth in a contemporary setting. They are usually, but not always, shadow worlds, which are covered in a later section.

The science fiction fantasy world is based on science that is not based on any type of real science, but simply conjured by the mind of the writer. Comic book stories are a good example of science fiction fantasy, as the characters often conduct science experiments that go wrong and cause a superhero or villain when there is absolutely so scientific proof behind the outcome of the experiment.

Science Fiction

Science fiction story worlds encompass more than outer space, although planets and other outer space locations, such as space stations, and asteroids are arguably the most popular. Robots, experiments with dire consequences, time travel, super computers, super plagues, and cyber and steam punk are all part of the science fiction genre. Government and religion will usually play a large role in a science fiction story as the moral issues and societal impacts brought about by the new technologies will be an underlying theme of the story.

Hard-core science-fiction aficionados want the science part to be as close to our known science as possible with reasonable postulates. The reader might allow some artistic license, but no reader will allow the author to play fast and loose with outrageous science that has absolutely no basis in fact. Those stories fall more into the fantasy world than the science fiction world.

Flying cars, space travel, time travel, transporters, sonic

showers, molecular restructuring for production of food and other materials, genetics, bionics, and nanotechnology are just a few of the many elements found in science fiction works. And while not all of them are based on scientific fact, most are generally accepted in the space opera subgenre of science fiction. For instance, travel at the speed of light or faster than the speed of light is deemed to be impossible, but it has become so ingrained in the culture of the science fiction world, readers will often overlook it. But not always. It's a good idea to check and double check the guidelines of the publisher and to read some of what the house publishes before submitting to discover which science fiction elements are allowed. This is also a good idea when considering any publisher, not only those publishers who deal with speculative fiction.

And speaking of space opera, here are some common mistakes to avoid when writing a story set in space. These are just a few, and it's a good idea to do a little research on bad movie science or bad movie physics. These critics of movie science can give great insight as to what signifies as good, bad, and indifferent science mistakes. As a matter of course, do a little research on any type of technology when contemplating its use in a story.

•   There is no air or oxygen in space; it is a vacuum. Therefore sound does not travel, and there are no flames. So, when the hero is on the deck of his ship and has launched the fatal attack, he will not hear the explosion of the enemy ship, nor will he see fire or flames. Even if it was a huge enemy ship filled with oxygen, the oxygen will dissipate too quickly to burn. However, he will see the flash from the explosion.

•   People and objects do not move slower in zero gravity. And a person in the center of a spin (such as to "create gravitational forces") will not feel the effects of the spin. If you want to test this, sit in the middle of a merry-go-round while it is moving.

•   A body will not instantly freeze or explode when exposed to the vacuum of space.

- Instant communication between humans and aliens without some sort of translation device is unbelievable.

Research isn't only for the space opera subgenre. Medical issues must be researched for a super plague. Steam engines and inventions of the Victorian era, such as the Babbage engine, should be researched for steampunk, as well as the dissenters of technology, commonly known as Luddites. A writer wanting to pen a cyberpunk novel should research computer technology, and a writer interested in extinction level events should research space phenomena, volcanoes, etc.

Shadow

A shadow world is one that exists in tandem with the real world, in real world locations, but is generally unknown to the human inhabitants. Vampire stories are usually set in shadow worlds. They have their own societies and walk among the humans, but the humans have no knowledge of their existence. Except, for instance, the vampire slayer.

A skillful writer can create a shadow world with almost any type of inhabitant and use almost any of the different story worlds to create the shadow world. Fairies are often written as having their own society, as are leprechauns, aliens, and werewolves (although the pack society is much smaller than that of a fairy society).

Humans with psychic abilities also fall into the category of a shadow world. The psychic's world is functionally different from the non-psychic's. Although psychics may work, play, live, and essentially be a part of society, their world remains hidden to the other inhabitants. When you can hear other people's thoughts, or enter other people's dreams, or move objects with a thought, you tend to keep it a secret. Fear is probably the best reason to keep the secret. Fear of being labeled a witch, demon, or freak, the fear of being forced into years of testing by the government, and the threat of other people fearing you are all good reasons not to tell others of special abilities.

Of course, some characters equate their ability with fame and fortune, and they don't allow those fears into their lives. They write books, do demonstrations, and appear on late-night television talk shows. Again, this is a world far different from the everyday life.

The skill needed to write an engaging shadow world lies in the blending of the story world with the real world while keeping them segregated enough to make the ignorance of the humans plausible.

Virtual Reality

A virtual reality is a world inside the confines of a computer-generated landscape. The inhabitants are depicted as avatars inside the VR, and they may be cartoonish or realistic. The VR landscape can be entered through a private or public terminal, or through a specially made VR device, such as a chair, or a set of VR goggles.

The landscape and scenery may appear warped, as if the visitor is looking at it through thick glass, or as some form of animation. The visitor will not be allowed outside the boundaries of the VR, nor will everyone and everything inside the VR interact with the visitor. The visitor must be vigilant though, because his contact in the VR may have chosen a tree as an avatar, or a sign, or a flower. Nothing in the VR world can be overlooked or dismissed. Everyone and everything is a potential enemy or a potential source of information.

One of the considerations for the virtual reality is how much the VR world affects the character whose physical presence is still in the real world. If the character is injured or dies in the VR, will he bleed or die in the real world? If the character falls in love with another VR character, can their love be sustained in the real world?

Another consideration is addiction. Will a character become

so addicted to the VR world that he doesn't disconnect to take care of basic human needs like food? And what happens if the character who refuses to leave the VR world remains "plugged in" to the point where the constant stimulation doesn't allow the mind to rest. Sleep deprivation causes a reduction in problem solving, a lack of creative thinking, and other brain function problems, and can cause hallucinations if the deprivation is severe. If the character in a VR world is fighting bad guys, or seeking information, the effects of sleep deprivation can be deadly, in the real world as well as the VR world.

Earth

Earth? Yes, Earth. Perhaps a settler from another planet has colonized on Earth, or a civilization has been living at the bottom of the ocean, or deep within the mountains of Tibet, or underground beneath the harsh landscape of the tundra? A postapocalyptic Earth, or any vision of Earth after some sort of war, plague, or natural disaster, will look and feel much different than it does now. Then there's always Atlantis, or any other mythical city that is perceived to be hidden somewhere on Earth.

Story worlds need to be built for these scenarios, with the limits of our physical world. The aliens will definitely have some technologies not yet discovered on Earth, as may the other hidden societies. However, in order to avoid detection, these societies will have a system in place for keeping their secrets hidden. They may not have any immunity built for the diseases that have developed on the surface of the planet or outside of their "protected" boundaries. They may have developed a disease for which the rest of Earth's inhabitants have no immunity. Food, clothing, dwellings, will be vastly different for the hidden societies than for the Earth as we know it.

If the inhabitants of a hidden society interact with the inhabitants of Earth, voluntarily or otherwise, they will bring pockets of their society with them. The air will be different for them, as will the taste of foods, the temperature, and for a character who has lived closer to the Earth's core, the force of gravity at the surface will feel different. All of these details should be taken into consideration.

A post-apocalyptic Earth may be highly contaminated by nuclear fallout, either from war or as a result from some sort of space event. A plague or epidemic may leave water, soil, and food contaminated with mutated strains of the disease from decaying bodies that were never properly buried or destroyed. Technology of the time probably won't work, either from destruction, or the lack of individuals who know how to operate it. Landscapes may be a heap of rubble, or bleak cities where only life was destroyed. Eventually, those cities left intact will become ghost towns or legends, perhaps a utopian place the characters try to find.

Time Travel

Time travel has fascinated the human race since the first person wished he/she could change something in his/her past. But if one event or outcome is changed, how does it affect the flow of time from that point forward? It is the paradox that time travel creates which fascinates us, such as "the grandfather paradox" that essentially asks, "If I go back in time and kill my grandfather before my father is born, will I exist?"

These stories can be science fiction, using postulates from known theories to effectuate the actual time travel, or they can be fantasies using magic or some other non-scientific means to achieve time travel.

The objective of the time travel can be anything. To right a wrong, to rediscover an ancient technology, to prevent or stop a war, or something as simple as sightseeing.

Like the alternate history story, the time travel story requires a bit of research, and cause and effect should be taken into consideration, especially when dealing with the time travel paradox.

Four
The Foundation

For any building project, you need a firm, solid foundation. From the words of a parable, the wise build on rock, and the foolish build on sand. Sand shifts and washes away with the rains and the tides, and the unstable foundation of sand almost guarantees your structure will fall. The structure built on rock will stand firm.

The same holds true for your story world. It needs a good foundation or it will crumble and wash away.

Choosing the Right Foundation

There are two common types of foundations: spread footing and slab. They are both made of concrete (a mixture of cement, which is an aggregate like limestone or granite) and fly ash or clay. When water is added to the cement, a chemical reaction takes place and causes the ingredients to form a bond. Once the concrete has hardened, it becomes solid and resistant to damage. Sometimes, rebar is added to reinforce its tensile strength.

In order to choose the right foundation, the builder needs to know the size of the structure. For a small structure, a spread footing foundation is needed. For a larger structure, a shallow depth slab foundation is needed. And for the largest structures, a deep slab foundation with reinforcing is needed.

- Flash fiction and short stories can stand on a foundation of spread footers.

- Novellas can stand on a foundation of spread footers or a slab foundation.
- Full-length novels can stand on a slab foundation.
- Series can stand on a deep slab foundation with reinforcements.

A writer should not place a short story on a deep slab foundation. Nor should a writer build a full-length world structure on footers. In other words, the writer only needs a minimal amount of world building for a short work of fiction, and a full-length novel will fall flat without enough world building. A series requires quite a bit of world building, but not all of it takes place in the first book. It may not all be revealed until the third, or fourth, or eleventh book. Some characters will see aspects of the world that others do not. Remember, the scope of a story world is directly tied to the characters' points of view, not the author's all knowing view from the mountaintop.

Laying the Foundation

The concrete of world building is the mixture of elements of the world the writer wants to build, such as certain magic or technologies, and the world's inhabitants. The story world is the cement and the inhabitants are the water that causes the change. The inhabitants are fluid. They will have, and will probably go through, several evolutionary changes. Wars, plagues, golden eras, dark ages, all of these will affect the inhabitants and cause change. However, once the bond is made, no matter the changes to the inhabitants or the physical world, it will still be what defines the story world.

Combining the inhabitants with their physical world, their history, and evolution is creating the mythology of the world. It doesn't need to be perfect, and it doesn't need to be detailed to the nth degree. Most of these details are for the writer, not the reader. Bits and pieces will probably be brought out in the story, but not in a year-by-year or century-by-century breakdown of events that made the main character what he/she is today. Things to consider:

- Are the inhabitants indigenous to the world?
- Were they conquerors?
- Were they explorers who got stranded?
- Were they slaves brought to the world?
- Were they colonists from another land, planet, or galaxy?

The tone of the story world also takes shape here. Atmosphere and mood are relayed to the reader through the attitudes, thoughts, actions, and dialogue of the characters coupled with the natural setting. Is the tone dark and sinister? Comical? Mysterious? Romantic? Satirical? Gothic? Being conscious of the tone at this stage of the writing will help insure consistency throughout as other elements of the story world are chosen. This is where the story bible can help immensely. It can be used to keep track of the colors, textures, and weather patterns, etc., that set the tone of the scenes and use them to paint the story setting.

Many world mythologies contain rituals that pertain to the changing of the seasons, and many of the rituals persisted when the beliefs changed. Whether this type of seasonal ritual exists in the mythology, seasons can bear an important role in the story world. The length of the seasons may help or impede the main character's goal. An abrupt end to a season could be the result of an angry deity, the beginning of an extinction-level event, nuclear fallout, or magical spell.

Developing weather patterns is somewhat complex, with many different variables to consider. I would suggest that unless the story demands unique weather patterns, the writer should stick with the familiar. A desert will be hot and arid, until nightfall when the temperatures drop to dangerously cold. Story worlds that are built close to a planet's equator will be hotter than those built toward the poles. A jungle will have daily periods of rain, snow will be almost non-existence in southern regions, and plains will flood with too much rain. If there is an abrupt change in the weather patterns, like those listed for seasons, a brief explanation is usually all that is needed.

Time on Earth is measured by intervals. A day equals one complete rotation of the Earth. A year equals one complete rotation of the Earth around the sun. The twenty-four hour day and the division of a year into months is man-made.

Not all societies will have time measurements, nor will they have linear time. Some societies may have the ability to control the flow of time, or travel in time. Some hours of the day may be thought more magical than others, like midnight.

There are many uses for time in speculative fiction. Time may be directly related to the character's destiny if it has been foretold that he is to meet his mortal enemy (and death) on a certain day at a certain time, and no matter how hard he tries not to be there, he cannot seem to escape it. The measurement of time can be an integral part of the story, or as simple as day and night.

The Cornerstone

Once the size of the structure has been determined and an appropriate foundation poured, a cornerstone must be laid. The cornerstone serves as a guide for the placement and position of the rest of the structure. The cornerstone of the story world is the main character(s). The main characters may be hero and heroine, hero/heroine and mentor, best friends, or mortal enemies. Everything else in the story world will relate to the cornerstone and be built in reference to the main characters and their relationships with each other.

The importance of the cornerstone character to the story world is paramount. Think about some of the characters who have stood out in speculative fiction works. One thing they all have in common is their passionate belief, even when the first glimpse of their worlds contradicts their convictions. Readers connect with characters who believe the aliens are hostile when the aliens haven't shown any violent behavior, or the time traveler who believes he can change things for the better, or the character who knows he can find the lost city, treasure, or astronaut. Readers connect because of the character's unfailing belief.

The idea of a strong cornerstone is also true from an intellectual standpoint. *Primum non nocere* (First, do no harm) can be considered the cornerstone of medicine. This sort of cornerstone idea can be related to the main character in the form of story theme. If the theme is revenge, the world builder needs to know why the character is seeking revenge. Then the builder must determine what in the story world will provide the opportunities to accomplish the goal, or present obstacles to keep the main character from obtaining the goal, and thus provide growth and conflict for the character. The obstacles could be physical, such as long distances, impassable mountains, etc., or they could be ideologies of the society such as the belief that obtaining revenge will bring sorrow to the avenger's family for seven generations, and the character will be forced to live and witness all of the sorrow he caused.

These are all parts of the weaving process the writer must learn to accomplish with ease. Using the physical story world to enhance the story's tone, theme, and plot, or the character's goal, motivation, and conflict is what makes the great stories memorable.

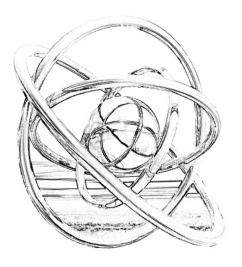

Five
The Exterior Walls, Floors, and Roofing

If you've ever shopped for carpet, hardwood, tile, or marble, you know flooring is a major decision and not something just to be walked over. It has to be strong enough and durable enough, to take wear and tear for years. The same holds true for the exterior walls and roofing. The decision to use brick, stone, logs, adobe, or wood for the exterior walls, and slate, tin, or shingles for the roofing, all play into the overall strength of the structure. In building a story world, these elements of the structure are government and military.

Government encompasses everything in the story world. Unfortunately, story world inhabitants can't escape from the government in their everyday lives any more than humans can. Like the inhabitants, the government may have gone through, or is going through, or there is the threat of it going through, a major change. However, the writer needs to choose the type of government, the different branches, the laws, the court system, the types of punishments meted out, the types of incarceration, and rehabilitation. This will also determine armies, allies and enemies, the type of spies, and any resistance movements.

Obviously, the more rigid the building material, the more rigid the form of government.

The story world may have one centralized government, or smaller governments each ruling their own part of the story world. It may be directly connected to the story world's religion, or it may develop solely from the need for order.

For flash fiction and short stories, and some novellas, the government may never be a story element, or anything more than a passing reference to the king, or president, etc. In full-length novels and series, it should be structured enough to provide reasoning and balance to the character's actions, non-actions, or point of view. In stories where morality is part of the theme, such as rapid growth of technology, or the banning of magic, the government, and religion, should be developed in detail.

Writers should research any form of government they intend to use as a model in a story world. I encourage this for two reasons. The first is because if a writer wants to create a story world government from the model of an established governmental system, the writer needs to know exactly how the government is structured. The second is because if a writer wants to break the rules, the writer must first know the rules. (This also applies to all "rules" of writing.) It's also a good idea to do more extensive research on governmental systems to create a unique governmental system for a story world.

On Earth, we have a variety of governments to use as a model for a story world. Some are recognizable and used in different parts of the world while others have long since vanished from the governmental landscape. These are very brief and broad descriptions of the governments listed on the world building worksheet.

- Anarchy
- Communism
- Democracy
- Dictatorship
- Egalitarian
- Feudalism
- Monarchy
- Oligarchy
- Republic
- Theocracy
- Totalitarian
- Tribal

Anarchy

Anarchy is a total lack of government. Think barbarism. There are no governmental controls of rules, no punishments, and no system to ensure that any task gets done for the common good. Some societies in the story world may start in anarchy or spiral down into anarchy as a result of war or some sort of natural disaster.

Communism

Communism is a form of government in which all individuals have equality. There are no officials. Each member of a communist society shares the work and the wealth. No one individual has more influence or power than another. This sort of system is appealing, but there are always complications.

Democracy

Democracy is a form of government in which the people elect the leaders. In a democratic republic, a representative is elected to represent the peoples' interests to the leaders. In theory, the representative would always cede to the majority of the individuals of the electorate. However, if an individual has more power, or money, or influence within the electorate, the representative will feel pressure to please that individual.

Dictatorship

A dictatorship is where one individual seizes and takes control of the government, usually with military force. The leader's word is final, and there is no consideration for the people of the society for which the dictator rules. Punishments are often swift, harsh, and inconsistent. Fascism is also a dictatorship that values nation or race over individual, and has strict control over economic and social structures.

Egalitarian

An egalitarian system of government declares all citizens equal in social stature, economic stature, etc., and is similar to the communist and socialism doctrines. A true egalitarian system is most often found in small governmental systems, like a village, tribe, or clan. Otherwise, giving every citizen an equal part of the whole is not feasible. Some contributions will always outweigh others, and this becomes more apparent in larger governmental systems.

Feudalism

Feudalism is a hierarchal form of government, usually royal. In return for military service, a lord grants land to a vassal, such as a knight. The vassal can then grant small parcels of his land to farmers, blacksmiths, weavers, etc. These workers give a large portion of their goods and services to the vassal, who in turn also gives a portion to the lord. It should be noted, though, that there are many different academic views of feudalism, and if a writer intends to use this system of government, a lot more research is necessary.

Monarchy

A monarchy is a form of government that revolves around royalty. A king or queen has absolute power in a monarchy. The children of the monarchs are the heirs to the power. The monarch may have advisors and will most often appoint law enforcement officials and judges to police different regions. This system of government is usually seen in high fantasy and secret societies.

Oligarchy

An oligarchy is a form of government in which the rich or elite rule. The oligarchs are usually a shadow government that controls the figure-head government such as a royal family, religious leader, or some other type. The children of the oligarchs expect to be heirs to the power.

Republic

A republic is similar to a democracy in that some or all parts of the government are representatives of the people. However, the president, chancellor, king, etc., may not hold the highest power. Those positions can be ceremonial or advisory. A counsel, or consul may be the highest power in a republic. A republic is one of the hardest government systems to write, because a peoples' perception of a republic varies as to the rules of a republic, the highest authority, and the breadth of governmental control.

Theocracy

A theocracy is a form of government that is controlled by a religion. The religious leaders determine laws, punishments, acceptable behavior, etc., by the tenets of the religion.

Totalitarian

A totalitarian system of government is similar to a dictatorship. The government controls every aspect of life for its citizens. The government controls all culture, such as what television and movies may be viewed, which religion may be practiced, which books may be read, etc. It may be from a totalitarian's own sense of morality or that of a religion. Contraband is dealt with swiftly and harshly.

Tribal

A tribal or clan society is usually a close-knit society in which many of the citizens have familial ties, most often from a common ancestor or god. True familial ties need not be present, as people can be accepted into the tribe/clan by performing a service or pledging their lives to the good of the tribe/clan. The chief or laird is the highest power and usually makes decisions on crime and punishment and tribe/clan activities.

For the purposes of the world building worksheet, the government need not be fully noted. If, for example, the writer decides on a monarchy system of government, only a few highlights need to be noted because most people know the basic way a monarchy works. However, if the writer decides to combine elements of different governments to create a system unfamiliar to the reader, more extensive notes will be needed.

When creating a totally new system of government, be...well, creative. If the story has a governmental system in which computers use logic sequences to decide on laws, how they are interpreted, trade agreements, elections, etc., then why not call it a computocracy? Or comparchy? The labels or titles a writer gives the system and its leaders, while sometimes strange or even comical, depending on the tone of the story, can relay as much information as a few detailed paragraphs on how the system works.

Walls and a roof also protect, or defend, the inhabitants of the structure from the elements, exposure, and attackers. They also provide a sense of security. This represents the military.

Some sort of military force is needed in every type of society. Otherwise, the society faces the possibility of being invaded and overtaken, or annihilated, by an aggressive society. The landscape of the story world and the type of government usually determines the type of military.

If the military is to play an integral role in a story, then special attention should be paid to the military, as it is usually a society unto itself. The hierarchy, or chain of command, should be established with a leader or leaders, officers, non-commissioned officers, and the rank and file.

Members may be drafted or conscripted, they may volunteer, or perhaps during wartime, prisoners are placed in the front lines with promises of freedom if they survive. There may be a special segment of the citizenry from which all soldiers or warriors are bred. Whatever the case, there will probably be some sort of induction ceremony, and another ceremony when a certain rank is achieved if moving up in rank is allowed. There will be some sort of recognition and decorations for honor, or bravery, or mastering a certain skill. There will be privileges that come with certain ranks.

A military will also have its own set of rules and regulations and a set of punishments for those who break them. The military court system will have its own rules, with military advocates and judges. In wartime, it may be no more than a kangaroo court, or mock trial, with no advocacy for the accused and with the outcome determined beforehand.

Just as a government must be funded, a military must also be compensated. There are many and various methods for a government to generate income, whether it is by taxes, tribute, or tithes. A portion of that income must be provided to the military forces. We've all heard the old saying that an army travels on its stomach. A hungry army will become a pack of marauders. An unpaid army will become mercenaries. The government will be faced with the task of providing food, weapons, uniforms, transportation, training, etc., for the warriors or soldiers, and money for expenses has to be generated through income.

If martial law is not in effect, then some other type of police force is necessary. It will also have a chain of command, specialized education, honors, and decorations like the military. Most often, a police force is governed locally and under the same laws as the citizenry. Police, as well as the criminals, will answer in a court of law. The way the court system functions will be determined by the type of government the writer has chosen.

This does not mean, however, that the local police force will always adhere to a certain code of conduct. Power corrupts, and widespread corruption may turn a local police force into something akin to a brute squad that terrorizes the citizens and uses a macabre caricature of the laws, along with their weapons, to enforce their power over the population.

The government may also have secret police, which quite naturally do not stay secret for very long. It is more a fear of the *idea* of you, or your family being taken from your home—beaten, drugged, or unconscious—to some underground facility by the secret police, than the act itself that keeps the average citizen from speaking out against the government.

Spy networks are the red headed step-children of the government. They belong to the government, but no governmental official wants to acknowledge their existence. Spies can be used to gather information and intelligence on another government, another army, or its own country's citizenry. If the government is based on technology or corporate entities, one branch may use spies to ensure the balance of power within the government, especially if there is tension between the different government branches.

Vigilante groups appear in places where there is no formal system of law, or in a city, town, or village that is so distant from the center of law and government it can't be policed by normal means. Unfortunately, it is often a case of good intentions turned bad. Citizens may start out with a vigilance committee, people who take it upon themselves to keep a watchful eye out for those in their community who break the rules or try to take undue advantage of situations. The vigilante group, left unchecked, will become tyrannical, and any slight or offense, according to the group's edicts, is dealt with harshly.

A vigilante group may also come to being by a few people who don't like the way the current law official handles a certain type of crime. These people don't need further proof, or a court of law to tell them a person is guilty, and by sheer force, they will exact punishment. Vigilante groups were common in the American west during the pioneer days and were motivated by greed and power. Unfortunately they also appeared in the South, which was motivated by prejudice. Vigilante groups can also be motivated by religion, or something more visceral, like starvation or lack of medical attention.

Six
The Electrical, Plumbing, and Heating & Air

Electrical lines, plumbing lines, and venting systems form a complex web throughout a building under the floors and in walls and ceilings. These conduits provide energy, water, cool air in the summer and warm air in the winter. They represent economy and education. And due to the fact that they are so interwoven with the floors, walls, and ceiling, they are most often a result of the type of government and/or societies created, or they are the basis of the government and/or societies.

However, just as the electrical lines are not one-size-fits-all, neither should the story world's education be accessible to, or wanted by, every inhabitant. Not all closets have lights, and you can't plug your toaster into a 220-volt receptacle. Some rooms will be illuminated with blinding overhead lights, while others may only have crude oil lamps. There are, of course, exceptions. The most common is a theocracy. The beliefs are forced upon the population, usually with violent or deadly consequences for those who refuse to accept the one and only recognized religion. However, in spite of the consequences, there are oftentimes dissenters.

Economy

The story world's economy will also stem from the system of government. Will the government use taxation to raise the money required to operate, or will it own all businesses, farms, manufacturing, etc., and provide for its citizens? Will it be a combination of economies, or one that provides for the elite from the taxation of the average citizen or vice-versa?

It is important to make logical choices concerning economies as they relate to the government. It is highly unlikely that a dictatorship will have a free market economy. Likewise, a democracy is not likely to have a spoils of war economic system. Any writer who creates a government should take as much care to create an economic system that complements the government. Does this mean a government and economic system that are incongruent cannot work in a story world? No, it doesn't. However, it takes great care and skill to make them believable.

As with governmental systems, our own history and present day systems provides a wealth of information on which to model an economic system. Some will be more familiar than others. Here are some very brief and broad descriptions of the economic systems listed on the world-building worksheet.

- Barter
- Free Market or Capitalist
- Corporate Owned
- Planned
- Socialism
- Spoils of War
- Tribute

Barter

A barter economy is a system in which food, goods, services, or information is traded for other goods, services, food, or information. This type of economic system is often seen in young governments, or established tribal/clan governments, and some feudalistic governments. Spy networks may also establish a bartering network, no matter the systems of government they encounter.

Free Market

A free market or capitalist economy is a system based on supply and demand. Producers are free to price their products based on what the market can bear with no interference from governmental agencies. There are no set prices, no price controls, and no protections against price gouging. A weaver can sell cloth to a merchant for one price and, in the next minute, sell the same amount of cloth of the same quality to the next customer for more or less money.

Corporate Owned

A corporate-owned economy is a system in which large corporations control every aspect of goods and services sold. The corporation will own the land on which food is grown, as well as the equipment, fertilizer, storage, etc., and will pay the farmer. The corporation can then set and control the price of the food. One corporation may have many subsidiaries that own and control many different industries, or each industry may be owned and controlled by a different corporation.

Planned

A planned economy is a system in which the government has control over the goods produced and control over the prices for goods and services sold. The government may look at its citizens and determine only a certain amount of wheat is needed and either force some wheat farmers to do something else or force others to become wheat farmers. The government looks at all natural resources and determines which may be used in production, such as coal for furnaces or trains, wood for building houses, gold for currency or jewelry, etc.

Socialism

Socialism is an economic system in which the government doesn't own or control the production of goods and services, but does control the distribution of those goods and services to its citizens. This system usually goes hand-in-hand with an egalitarian system of government or a communist system of government. Every citizen is equal in voting stature, social stature, and wealth.

Spoils of War

A spoils of war economic system is common for a warrior society. The warriors may have a home base, but they are generally nomadic, traveling to their next conquest. The warriors take what they need and want from the people they conquer, sell or trade what they do not want, and may send a portion to their home base.

Tribute

A tribute economic system is similar to a spoils of war system. An invading army takes a city or region by force, but leaves as much of the infrastructure as possible. The invaders appoint positions that are filled by their countrymen, and these overseers insure that a certain amount of money, or goods and services, or both is paid in tribute to the victor. Sometimes one government will demand tribute from a weaker government prior to invading, with the promise that the weaker government will not be invaded, or with the promise that it will protect the weaker government from other invaders.

Education

With a government in place, and an economic system in place, the next major part of the story world that affects the characters is the educational system.

The character only knows what he is taught. As with point of view, the characters do not share in the omniscience of the writer. Learning, growing, and changing are all part of the character's journey through the story.

The type of government and economic system usually determines the kind of education a character receives. An egalitarian government may provide the same education to every child. A free market economic system may only provide the level of education commensurate with the family income. A theocracy will provide an education based on the religious beliefs and will not introduce theories, magics, or other curricula that are in contrast to those religious beliefs.

Social position within a society may determine the educational opportunities. Those of a higher status, such as a peer of the realm, will receive a better education than the peasants. A prince will probably learn a great deal in science, mathematics, diplomacy, warfare, justice, and hunting, but may not know how to field dress an animal for eating, or how to grow crops.

A character who has had a proper academic education may not understand the need for games. A character who expects to spend his life as a laborer may not want to learn to read.

A leader who wants to enslave a society, or a specific sector of a society, will probably outlaw any type of education. A conquering society may do the same. Restricting or denying education takes away a major component of freedom from those being suppressed or enslaved.

For specialized characters, such as vampires, some abilities may exist at birth, but the character will need to learn how to use the ability. He may have a knack for dematerializing with almost no instruction, but fails at completely removing a human's memory even after years of trying.

Also, for specialized characters who have magical or psychic abilities, they may be able to acquire knowledge by reading someone's mind or connecting with an object. Not all knowledge is learned through study and education.

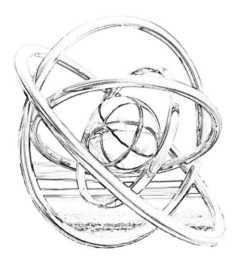

Seven
The Ceiling

The ceiling is an interesting piece of architecture. It is aesthetically pleasing, as its patterned plaster, or tiles, hide the ugly maze of pipes, wires, and vents from our view. It also provides a bit of protection by filtering some sounds, and keeping inhabitants dry when there is a leak in the roof. The ceiling represents religion, or a belief system, whether or not it has a supernatural deity.

Religions can originate from a number of different scenarios. There are primitive religions and belief systems, such as sun worshippers, where religion started as a way to explain supernatural or scientific concepts primitive cultures could not understand. Organized religions are based on the teachings of a spiritual being. Cults can idolize anything in the universe, and other belief systems can be based on magic, science, or nature.

The one thing a religion or belief system needs is people who believe with enough force or influence to propagate the belief. This can be accomplished by either the performance of a miracle, or the charismatic ability of a prophet, disciple, priest, or mystic to persuade others to join them in worship.

In the case of a cult or some other insular group, the actual membership may be small and remain segregated outside of normal society. Depending on the belief system of the cult, their "holy land" could be a commune or a compound.

However, whether it is a state religion, free religion, cult, sun worshipper, etc., rituals will play a large part in the experience. The rituals may include fire or water for cleansing and purification, blood for sacrifice, wine or hallucinogenic drugs to free the spirit from the body or to allow those participating to hear the words of a prophecy.

This is also the part of the story world where taboos, superstitions, and traditions will develop, either from fear of a religious figure, fear of the government, or lack of education.

Superstitions will also probably long outlive their believability. It is believed that knocking on wood dates back to ancient times when people thought good spirits lived in trees.

Some superstitions have subtle changes from region to region. What happens if your palm itches? If my left palm itches, nothing happens, but if my right palm itches, I can expect money to come my way. Others will tell you if their left palm itches, they expect to lose money. Even within a small group of people, a few of them will have a different interpretation of itchy palms.

Then there are colloquial superstitions that haven't traveled far from their origins. I've always heard that if you count the number of train cars while stopped at the track, that will be the number of days until someone in your family dies. Yet, I have seldom heard of this superstition outside of my community.

The same concepts hold true for taboos and traditions. A world or society with religious influences will probably have superstitions and taboos dealing with demons and devils. A world or society that lacks education may have a monthly ceremony with offerings of their finest crops to the sky so the good rain will continue to come. A world or society based on technology may consider it taboo to own a pencil.

There may also be taboos concerning sex. No signs of affection, like holding hands or kissing, in public. Perhaps sex is only allowed on certain days of the month, or when a couple is trying to have a baby. Rape could be a heinous crime, or it could be seen as a man's right. Oral sex, or other types, may be outlawed. Or taboos can travel into the outrageous. It might be against the law or religion for someone with blonde hair to marry or have sex with someone with red hair or green eyes. Or maybe only two people who are the same height can have sex.

This is definitely a subject the writer can have fun with, especially if building a world where a warrior society plays a major role in the story. To breed the strongest and best fighters of the species, rules and taboos regarding sex will have an impact. They will also have an impact on any society in which certain traits, such as intellect, artistic ability, strength, or looks are revered over others.

Many superstitions and taboos have remedies that will negate the consequences. Spill some salt? Throw a pinch over your left shoulder. Break a mirror? Bury it under the moonlight. So, in dealing with superstitions and taboos, writers should think not only of the origins and consequences but also of the out clauses.

Traditions can appear in many ways. Wedding and funeral traditions are probably the most common, but traditions can be woven into a story at almost any event. The birth of a child, the gathering of crops, buying or building a house, receiving a new weapon, and completing a level of education can be associated with some type of tradition.

Holidays are also traditions—a time set aside, whether it be a day, a week, or longer, for feasts, recreation, remembrance, etc. Perhaps weddings can only occur on a certain holiday. A serious and staid society may have a holiday when atavistic behavior emerges, either by choice or because it is brought about by some genetic anomaly or supernatural force.

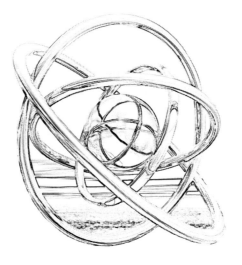

Eight
Doors and Windows

In the story world structure, doors and windows represent technologies, magic, and culture. Windows allow illumination, in the form of science, ideas and imagination, to enter the structure. Doors allow guests to enter and exit, and those guests may bring new ideas, new technologies, new arts and culture into the structure. Doors and windows are also risky, as it is through those same elements a burglar may enter and steal ideas and technologies. Or, someone disguised as a guest may actually have malicious intent.

A guest may also innocently introduce some idea, form of art, or technology to the inhabitants that the government or religious leaders are trying to keep out. A dark age period occurs when all the doors are kept shut and the windows are kept covered. A golden age occurs when the doors and windows are kept open and a great flow of technological or other type of advancement takes place.

Technology, magic, and culture develop over a long period of time, and like education and religion may only be available to the government or a select class within society. For example, government farms may have state of the art machinery, while the ordinary citizen is only allowed a horse-drawn plow.

If the writer decides on a peaceful, utopian world in which the inhabitants are centered solely on culture and philosophy, there is the risk of the world being easily conquered. If a world is based on magic, there is the risk of losing magical ability to technology. If a world is technology based, there is the risk of it destroying itself. No one method is perfect, and magic may lead to technology, or technology may lead to more leisure time to pursue art and culture. Or, there may be a mixture.

Technology

Technology is fluid and changes with the needs, discoveries, and natural resources of the story world. Very few technologies are discovered through a "eureka" moment or by accident. There is a logical path to founding technologies. Clothing for the story world probably started with animal skins, then to a cloth once the inhabitants discovered a way to sheer the sheep, spin thread, and then weave it into cloth. However, it was probably rough against the skin, tore easily, and didn't last very long. So, a better loom was built for a stronger, better weave, then dyes were added for different colors. From there, more raw materials provide different types of materials, some better, prettier, or more expensive to weave than others. Patterns and fashions emerged from the prettier, more expensive cloths, and in a matter of a hundred years or so, the poorer classes are fated to wear the lower quality materials while the richer classes wear silk. Once demand for more clothes, and even better quality comes about, machines are developed.

The things to remember regarding technologies are the basic needs of the inhabitants. Food, clothing, shelter, medicine, defense, and the availability of raw materials (animals, vegetables, fruits, wood, herbs, copper, iron, etc.) to fill those needs will determine the types of technologies that will logically come about as the civilization grows. Resist the temptation to have technologies in the story world that appear illogical or ahead of their time. Lost technologies might be found as a quest element of the story, but the inhabitants are probably not going to immediately understand them or know how to use them.

Magic

Magic may be inborn or taught, but even if the magic is inborn, the skill must be developed. Children must be taught the laws of the magic they control. Are any types of magic outlawed or forbidden? Are all individuals taught to perform the same levels of magic? Is there something genetically, environmentally, or magically that controls how far an individual may advance in his skill? Is magic skill connected only to the strength of the mind, or to the strength of body as well? Does the magic evolve with the needs of the world? Can new magic be developed? Can magic be taken away, stripped, or restrained as punishment?

An important note to remember about magic. It isn't completely devoid of technology. Before the flying carpet is loaded up and taken on vacation, we look again at the cloth example. The knowledge of how to sheer wool from a sheep and produce thread from the wool must be understood, as well as how to dye the thread and then weave it into cloth. The method of manufacturing must be known before it can be duplicated in magic. Many times, magic and technology will develop concurrently and diverge when a society decides one is more important than the other.

There are, of course, exceptions. The ability to fly, or to become invisible, might be inborn magic. In writing a world where magic is predominant, it behooves the writer to decide which magic skills and abilities are natural to the inhabitants and which are learned.

The Healing Arts

It's easy to forget the healing arts—until a character in the story requires medical attention. Sometimes an author gets lucky and a physician, witch doctor, or shaman is the obvious choice of healer for the story line. And sometimes it is not clear how an injured character can be healed. If the character has travelled from his homeland where the medical arts are directly related to the technology, would the character look for a doctor? Probably, but what the character finds is perhaps closer to the witch doctor or some other sort of magical healing the character will not want to trust.

Specialized characters will require specialized healing arts. A vampire, werewolf, or alien who is injured cannot be taken to a conventional hospital. Not only will their injuries appear strange to contemporary doctors, but the doctors will have no way to determine a treatment. Perhaps antibiotics are poisonous, or snake venom is a pain killer. A little forethought to the healing arts can prevent an author from having to make a sudden stop in the story in order to work it out.

Culture

Culture will grow out of a combination of religion, technology, and/or magic. Pretty and handsome are culturally developed concepts, as are art, music, and even eating habits. Myths, legends, and fairytales are cultural elements. The appropriate way for men and women to wear their hair, to dress, to speak, and to act in each other's presence are cultural elements. Proper etiquette, in public and in private, will all be born of the story world's culture. Is eating in public a taboo? What about showing your teeth, your ears, your knees? Is whistling considered to be an invitation to fight? If you kiss someone of the opposite sex on the cheek, is it a sign of engagement?

When developing story world culture, does it need to be diverse or stringent? Will the emperor or religious leader always decide what is culturally acceptable, or will culture and customs develop solely from the inhabitants? Are there different cultural standards for the different classes of society? What are the punishments for ignoring the cultural restrictions? Banishment, penance, community service, jail, death?

Infrastructure

This is also where the story world's infrastructure will take shape. Technology, aesthetics, and raw materials will determine the roadways, the shape and height of buildings, the traffic system, the types of energy available for items like vehicles and other forms of transportation (land, water, and air), appliances, and communications.

In addition, recreation and types of entertainment—concerts, plays, movies, television, exhibits, sporting events, paintings, books, etc., will begin here and evolve as the story world's societies evolve.

Social Classes and Societies

Just as the interior walls of a structure form different types of rooms, the interior walls of the story structure form different types of social classes and societies. The elite will be separated from the poor. The armies will be separated from the general population. The rich and famous will have a different societal circle than the laborer. Political figures will also have their own social class.

Plan the social classes carefully. As an example, a house needs a number of rooms to be comfortably functional: a kitchen, living room (or great room), bedrooms, bathrooms, closets, laundry, etc., all proportionate to the inhabitants' needs. Equate social classes with the function, but not necessarily the size, of the corresponding rooms. The elite may equate to an opulent master bedroom. The famous may equate with the great room, where they can be seen and admired by all. The white-collar society may have a den or modest bedroom. The laborers may equate to the kitchen or laundry. If the world has slaves or serfs, they may equate to the closets, or garages.

Hallways are the connectors. The social classes must interact with each other, and societies from different worlds must interact with each other. The farmer must get his food to the market or grocer, who in turn sells it to the cook. The hallways may be short or long, wide or narrow, depending on how much interaction the writer needs between the social classes and societies. Some hallways may even be blocked.

These corridors will also determine commerce. Is gold or some other precious stone or metal the legal tender of the different societies? Or, does one society use gold while another society uses the barter system? Do the societies trade goods and services with each other? How do they determine the trade value from one system of commerce to another?

As a civilization develops, so will its social classes. Unfortunately, some sectors of society will always be poor while others are rich. Some are fated to be workers while others are fated to be thinkers, artists, priests, or leaders.

How these different social classes interact with each other is the element that brings life to the story. Despite the fact that the societies may disdain each other, they will be inter-dependent and rely on members of their own society as well as others to retain the level of social status they have acquired.

Money may decide the difference in the societies, or intelligence levels, or artistic ability, or fighting ability. Tailor the classes within the societies to the story world and don't throw in a class or society just to make a social statement. For instance, in a utopian society, the classes may go from good to best, without a poor class of people, while in a dystopian society, they may go from apathy to worst without a moral class of people. This doesn't mean an individual won't be poor or moral within those societies, only that there won't be a large segment of the population that fits the definition of poor or moral. Also, jealousies, prejudices, and other types of hate based on differences, or some perceived wrong, or perceived inferiority/superiority will emerge.

Each society in the story world will have its own social classes. The elite may not interact with the working class, unless or until some story element forces them to work together. However, it is almost impossible to truly segregate the classes. After all, it is the working class family who will pay to see the famous actor on stage, thus insuring the actor will remain elite. The rich will most likely have servants or slaves. Scientists will have assistants, or possibly sentient specimens. Starship pilots will have a crew.

A common story element is the ability of a character to rise above the social station to which he was born, so plan social classes and their interactions carefully.

The protagonist may or may not fit into the social class of his birth. It makes for great conflict when a peacemaker is born into a warrior class, or a scientist is born into a religious class.

And just as each society will have its own social classes, each world will have its own society.

Building only one society in a story world has the advantage of not having to maintain a lot of details, but most story worlds will require at least two vastly different societies. In order to make them interact, the writer must build corridors, or portals, through which they interact.

This means first and foremost, the societies must find a way to communicate. This may come as a shock, but not all foreign/alien societies speak English with a British accent. Therefore, the writer needs a path of communication before anything else. This doesn't mean the writer must create a language and add it to the written page, but some reference must be made to different dialects, languages, etc. Or, the universal translator device, mechanical or magical, should be close by.

A note about languages. One to ten words and/or phrases from a made-up language within the prose is acceptable if the meaning of the words can be discerned from the text. However, writing whole paragraphs or even a few sentences in a made-up language can be irritating to the reader. If a 50-page glossary is needed to give definitions for the language used in the story, it is probably too much. As writers, we love words and like to make up the languages our characters speak. However, for any writer who feels it necessary to compile an entire language, I suggest that it be a special project for the author's website, or a companion book for a series, other than trying to wow the reader with linguistic skills.

Once communication has been established, trading routes can be negotiated, arranged marriages can take place, and competitions can be arranged, athletic, artistic, or scientific. Diplomats will need to be trained and embassies built.

Some of the different societies' traditions, beliefs, taboos, and histories can be similar, but some will clash. Will the differences be enough to spark a feud? A war? Will two or more societies overlook their differences to unite against a common threat, be it an enemy society, a hoard of dragons, a plague?

Nine
Geography

Humans and humanoids require water to live, so most early colonists and pioneers settled near large bodies of water. However, if the character is rock-like and requires lava, an active volcano would be the prime real estate. When considering the geography of a story world, it is wise to plan a little bit. Serendipity is suspect in fiction. An accidental discovery of a needed resource provokes doubt. If purple water is needed in the magic potion during the climax, its discovery should be noted and then dismissed somewhere in the beginning of the story. This is similar in concept to if there's a gun on the mantle in Act I, it must go off in Act III.

Some writers use maps, while others depend solely on the cinematic view in their mind's eye.

For novels in which the story, or parts of the story, takes place in a historical period, such as Regency England, maps can usually be found.

Or, the basic outlines of ancient maps can be used for boundaries of the fictional world. Archipelagos can be added to existing maps (whether contemporary or ancient), boundaries can be moved, mountains and rivers can be added or deleted. And don't forget more interesting geographical features. Volcanoes, geysers, underground lakes and waterfalls, an oasis, salt lakes, tar pits, craters, and quicksand are some uncommon elements a writer might incorporate into the geography of the story world.

A Special Note About Geography

A planet with only one climate, such as a water planet, or an ice planet, or a desert planet, is extremely implausible. While it may make for great visual effects in movies, the effect in literature is less than stunning. A civilization would need to be small, a settlement or colony perhaps, in order to survive on such a planet as the raw materials needed to maintain a civilization would be scarce. Settlers with terraforming capabilities might be able to colonize a small parcel of land and thrive on such a planet, but a large population of say, boat dwellers, is unlikely. Where did they get the materials to build boats? And how did they manage evolutionary change without drowning or adapting to the water? Exactly; they wouldn't have. They would have evolved to a species that lives in the sea.

With the inherent problems of creating a believable evolution for humanoid characters on a one-climate planet, it is advisable for the writer not to attempt it.

One exception, and isn't there always an exception, is a natural disaster or an angry deity that causes a once lush multi-climate planet to become a one-climate planet. Still, the inherent difficulties of preparedness of the inhabitants, if they have time to prepare, and the coping mechanisms needed for survival in such a new environment are difficult hurdles for the writer to overcome. The basics—food, water, shelter, clothing, and medical issues—must all be addressed. From there, the need for order or fear of future retribution by the deity will bring about a system of government, etc. The world building in this case all happens on the written page.

For those writers who are visual, or for any writer who just needs a little visual stimulation to help with the landscaping, there are some great websites. Google's Sketch Up (www.sketch-up.com) has tools for drawing a city block, a district, or a whole city in 3D. A search for fantasy art can provide some great inspiration, as well as searches for pictures of jungles, the Antarctica, deserts, ghost towns, strange architecture, and outer space.

Ten
Decorations

Once the structure is complete, it's time to add the finishing touches—the furniture, the wall hangings, the knick-knacks, all of the decorative pieces added to a home. This is the point at which the writer decides on clothing, jewelry, status symbols for the social classes and societies, hairstyles, plants, pets, food, drink, toys, games, etc.

These are the specific descriptions that will connect the reader to the story. The universalisms. The homey touches each of the readers will use to identify with the story world and the characters.

A bed is a bed in any setting. It may be soft or made of stone, but it is still a place to sleep. The same holds true for other furniture, as well as things like forks, stoves, lamps, clothing, and transportation. All of these items have the same basic function, no matter the society or world in which they are used. Use vivid descriptions of these types of everyday items to connect the reader to the story world the same way vivid descriptions are used in bringing the fantastic elements of the story world to life.

Writing detailed description is hard. The words should paint a recognizable picture in the readers' minds without boring them to tears. And it should be done on the sly. It isn't wise to have characters remark on everyday objects just to bring them to the reader's attention. Don't write about the strange shape or style of a coffee mug, have one character throw it at another character, or into a fireplace. An exotic, intricate hairdo is boring, unless it's falling apart in a love scene, or floating in icy cold water in a death scene. In other words, make the details active and part of the story.

The Finished Product

Combining the story world with the characters and plot takes a little practice. The beginning writer may be tempted to write pages and pages of story world history and description to explain the actions of the characters. This sort of information dump doesn't advance the story. As I mentioned at the beginning, elements of the story world need to be woven like the threads of a tapestry.

Ease readers into the story world in such a way that they don't realize they've crossed the threshold from realty to fantasy. Leave a trail of breadcrumbs for them to follow and provide the pertinent story world elements through action and dialogue.

Don't rely on a well-crafted story world to carry a thin plot, or a well-crafted plot to stand on a skeletal story world. It takes both to create a story readers will remember.

Eleven
Scene Management

The devil is in the details. Keeping track of a character's eye color, hair color, and sometimes their name, in any piece of fiction is a daunting task. Even the bestsellers sometimes change a character's detail in the middle of the book. In a speculative fiction work, the number of details is doubled or tripled, and harder to remember. As I mentioned earlier, the story world bible is great for the noting of such details.

I am not a plotter by nature, and for me most plotting tools sound great in theory, but I struggle with the application. However, scene management, as it pertains to world building, is a tool that incorporates a little bit of plotting with story world mapping.

For scene management, use poster board, notebook paper, numbered note cards, a wiki, or whatever works with your writing style. Blocks drawn on the poster board or paper represent the different scenes in the novel. If using note cards, the numbers will correlate to the scenes. If using a wiki, each page will correlate to a scene. The method is similar to story boarding, except for the information.

With this method, the first step is the setting; ancient Egypt, a space craft, a laboratory, etc.

The second step is the visceral information. Add details like dark or light, hot or cold, snow, rain or sunshine, engine sounds, the scent of sanitizers, the grit of sand in the character's eyes or boots, anything that breathes life into the setting.

The third step is to add the details like the purple water needed for the potion, and the other clutter found in the scene environment and the mood or tone. A carnival, with its dancing lights, loud music, fast rides, games of chance, and strange characters might be great fun for one character while another character might find the same scene creepy or sinister.

The fourth step is to add the action. Does the character start in scene, enter the scene, or exit the scene? Does the character leave an object, take an object, or simply observe? Items such as clothing, sunglasses, weapons, purses, wallets, backpacks, etc., move through the setting with the character. Use the map to make sure the knife in the character's hand at the beginning of the scene doesn't magically move to a sheath in the character's boot at the end of the scene. Or that a piece of clothing torn in a fight doesn't magically repair itself in the next scene.

The fifth, and final, step is to add the directing signs. They can either be for the writer's reference, or for mapping the characters' movements. For the writer's reference, it could be a quick note that the character needs to go through the howling forest before he crosses the river. For mapping the characters' movements, it could be that the character found the purple water, but dismissed it. Instinctively, the reader will know it has some importance, but the need for purple water isn't immediate. Perhaps the immediate need of the character was a clue to the location of a magic sword. The directing signs should lead the reader to the next logical setting, either to find another clue or to find the sword. It may not be the next scene, but even if it is three or four scenes later, the reader will have no problem keeping up because of the directing signs.

Steps can be added as they are needed. Perhaps a character in the story is morphing, or showing symptoms of a disease. Perhaps the oceans are evaporating, or the ice caps are melting. A writer can make sure of a logical progression of these events using scene management.

Does all this scene management stuff sound a little like plotting? It is, in a way. Although it doesn't have the growth of the characters, or the events of each scene, it does give the writer some idea of where the story is going. It is also proof that story and story world are intertwined, and that everything in the story relates to the story world.

Appendix A
World Building Worksheet

Use a notebook or word processor to copy the information in this appendix, then build your world!

The Landscape:

What type of world is being built?
What is the tone, mood, atmosphere, of the World?
Will it encompass a universe, a country, a region, a city, or a neighborhood?

The Foundation:

What length is the story?
What type(s) of citizen will populate this world ?

Mythology of the World:

How was the world created/formed?
Have there been any major wars, plagues, natural disasters, etc, that have had an impact on the society, its growth, or evolution so that the effects are inherent to the story?

The Floors, Walls, & Roof:

Will the government be a major factor in this story?

If so, what is the core model of the government?

- Monarchy
- Democracy
- Republic
- Communism
- Theocracy
- Oligarchy
- Dictatorship
- Socialism
- Feudalism
- Totalitarianism
- Tribal/Clan
- Anarchy
- Other (describe)

Does the government control trade?
What is the government's war policy?
What is the government's diplomacy policy?
Have embassies been built?
Are there secret police or other secret government agencies?
Is there a spy network?
Does the government control births, deaths, marriages?
If so, what are the criteria?
How does the court system work?
Will the military play a role in the story?
Describe the hierarchy of the military, the different branches, how the military is compensated, how advancement within the ranks is achieved, and any laws that only relate to military personnel.

The Electrical/Plumbing/Heating & Air:

Does religion play a vital or pivotal role in the story?
Is there a central religion, state religion, or religious freedom?
Describe the religion(s):

What type of economic system(s) does the world have?

- Capitalist
- Free Market
- Planned
- Spoils of War
- Tribute
- Barter
- Corporate Owned
- None
- Other (describe)

What type(s) of currency is/are used?

What type of educational system does the world have?

- Free to All
- Government controlled
- Religion controlled
- Only to the rich
- Only to royalty
- Only to religious leaders
- Private institution only
- Specialized (testing for match, science, etc. to determine education)
- Through apprenticeship, indentured servitude, etc.
- Other (describe)

Taboos, superstitions, and traditions that have developed from government mandate, religious mandate, or lack of education:

The Doors & Windows:

What technologies have developed?
What technologies are needed?
Are any technologies banned or outlawed?
What types of magic are present?
What spells or abilities are needed?

Are any magical abilities banned or outlawed?

Remembering story tone and theme, what types of art are permitted?

Remembering story tone and theme, what types of art are not permitted?

Are there any great artists, philosophers, prophets, or leaders (past or present) who have an impact on the world?

The Rooms: Class Segments

Rate each segment from 1 to 10 in the percentage of the population.

Rate each segment from 1 to 10 by its power within the population

- Royal
- Government workers
- Politicians
- Aristocracy
- Scientific
- Religious
- Medical
- Educators
- Administration (private industry)
- Banking
- Business/shop keepers
- Military
- Law enforcement
- Criminal
- Factory workders
- Artists
- Sports/athletes
- Farmers/food producers
- Laborers
- Servant/service industry

- Slaves
- Sports figures
- Other
- Other
- Other

Specialized Segments:

Rate each segment from 1 to 10 in the percentage of the population.

Rate each segment from 1 to 10 by its power within the population

- Wizards/witches
- Fairies
- Weres
- Vampires
- Dragons
- Shapeshifters
- Psychics
- Symbiotes
- Mages
- Priests
- Demons
- Angels
- Aliens
- Gods and Goddesses
- Ghosts/spirits
- Other
- Other

The Geography:

Remembering the tone and theme of the world, write a brief description of the physical landscapes that will be used in this world. Include roadways, bodies of water, space/sky, architecture, sacred buildings, graveyards, plants, animals, colors, textures, temperatures, smells, etc.

What are the modes of travel?

The Decorations:

Remembering story tone & theme, and what types of technology, magic, and art are allowed/banned, describe the following: (for example, in a theocracy, it may be that only religious symbols can be used for decoration on public buildings, or even in private homes.)

Clothing, Hairstyles, jewelry:
Food & drink (include delicacies, aphrodisiacs, alcohol, forbidden, etc.):
Architecture:
Domestic animals/pets:
Furniture:
Weapons:
Tools:
Music, writings, paintings:
Magical objects:
Drugs, crimes:
Sports, games:

Appendix B
Suggested Reading and Other Resources

Suggested Reading:

The Writers Journey: Mythic Structure for Writers, by Christopher Vogler

World-Building A writer's guide to constructing star systems and life-supporting planets, by Stephen Gillett and Ben Bova

How to Write Science Fiction & Fantasy, by Orson Scott Card

The Writer's Complete Fantasy Reference, by Writers Digest

Giants, Monsters, and Dragons: An Encyclopedia of Folklore, Legend, and Myth, by Carol Rose

A Field Guide to Demons, Fairies, Fallen Angels and Other Subversive Spirits, by Carol K. Mack and Dinah Mack

Dictionary of Angels: Including the Fallen Angels, by Gustav Davidson

The Dictionary of Imaginary Places: The Newly Updated and Expanded Classic, by Alberto Manguel

The World of Darkness, by White Wolf Game Studio

World of Darkness: Armory, by Clayton Oliver, Keith Taylor, and Chuck Wendig

Websites:

Google Sketchup – http://sketchup.google.com/
Google Notebook - http://google.com/notebook
Wet Paint Free Wiki - http://www.wetpaint.com/
PBWiki Free Wiki - http://pbwiki.com/
Fantasy Art - http://www.elfwood.com
Fantasy Art II - http://www.fantasygallery.net
Antarctica Pictures - http://www.aad.gov.au/default.asp?casid=24039
Landscapes - http://www.outdoor-photos.com
Space Pictures - http://hubblesite.org/gallery

Note: Always check copyright information before using any picture from a website for personal use

Games:

Sid Meier's Civilization IV
Dungeons & Dragons
World of Darkness
Magic the Gathering
Final Fantasy
King's Quest

Note: Please do not use the stories created in a game situation for a novel. Readers of speculative fiction will recognize this. Instead, use them to experiment with theme, mood, and character development.

About Author Jessie Verino

Jessie began writing in the third grade—with a Halloween short story. She always enjoyed reading, especially historical romance, about all the wonderful worlds of eras gone by. Soon she discovered science fiction, and her writing has been influenced by both classic and current paranormal and sci-fi television shows and movies.

She lives in East Tennessee, close to the Great Smoky Mountains, and would never consider making her home anywhere else. Jessie loves Mexican food, pro football, and coffee. She's a member of the Smoky Mountain Romance Writers. SMRW is the East Tennessee RWA chapter.

Visit her on Facebook: http://www.facebook.com/JessieVerino

CPSIA information can be obtained at www.ICGtesting.com
Printed in the USA
BVOW010850041112

304575BV00006B/53/P